ADVANCED
ROCK BASS

FOR 4-, 5-, AND 6-STRING BASSES

BY MARK MICHELL

T0066246

Recording Musicians:
Mark Michell: Bass
Sean Ashe: Guitars
J.C. Bryant: Drums

To access video and audio visit:
www.halleonard.com/mylibrary
Enter Code
5222-3492-8430-9915

Cover photo: Brett Cullen

ISBN 978-1-4950-0899-3

HAL•LEONARD®
CORPORATION
7777 W. BLUEMOUND RD. P.O. BOX 13819 MILWAUKEE, WI 53213

In Australia Contact:
Hal Leonard Australia Pty. Ltd.
4 Lentara Court
Cheltenham, Victoria, 3192 Australia
Email: ausadmin@halleonard.com.au

Visit Hal Leonard Online at
www.halleonard.com

Table of Contents

Introduction

Hello, my name is Mark Michell. Welcome to my instructional book and accompanying video! I'll be discussing and demonstrating numerous techniques, approaches, and concepts that will help to unlock your creative potential on the bass. I find that creativity itself cannot be taught, but equipping yourself with the right tools will always yield a better outcome. As a bass player, more often than not, you will have more creative freedom than any other instrument when playing in an ensemble. This enables you to drastically control the outcome and feel of a given song.

Over the years, I've noticed a common trend in a majority of bass players: the feeling of being trapped in the root note, and wanting to do much more with the bass, but not knowing how. I find the three most common roadblocks that these players face are being unfamiliar with the notes on the fretboard, basic music theory, and not knowing exactly what role to choose in the context of a song as a bass player. Learning these three essentials will provide you with options, and having options allows you to create the perfect part. Understand that playing just the root note is indeed the perfect part sometimes—and there is nothing wrong with simplicity—but occasionally a song may require you to go beyond the root note. In this case, it's always better to have options to choose from, rather than having no options and wishing you did. The content in this book and accompanying video will offer perspective and provide all of the fundamentals necessary for you to build a better bass line.

About the Author

Since buying his first bass in 2004, Mark Michell has since splashed into the scene with his vast résumé of creative and educational endeavors. He has recorded bass for six studio albums to critical acclaim with the band Tetrafusion, solo artist Chris Letchford, and international recording/touring act Scale the Summit. His three most recently-recorded albums were released to Billboard-charting acclaim in the Top 200, Top Rock Albums, Top Independent Albums, Heatseekers Albums, Top Current Albums, and Contemporary Jazz Albums categories.

With years of collegiate jazz experience, dozens of tours under his belt, magazine press features and appearances through popular music video outlets AudioTree and EMG TV, Michell has established his role as one of the newest driving forces in the bass community. Coupled with his creative work, his educational offerings have served as an accessory to his love for music. Since 2011, Michell has been teaching full-time to students around the globe and offering live clinics on tours to hundreds of students. In recent years, he has published four instructional and tablature books for bass. Mark currently resides in his hometown of Shreveport, Louisiana with his wife and two children.

CHAPTER 1

UTILIZING THE FULL FRETBOARD

Sliding Exercise for C—Step #1:

 0:00–2:53

Sliding Exercise for C—Step #2:

 2:53–5:03

For Step #3, add a metronome to Step #2 and establish a working tempo.

Sliding Exercise for G—Step #1:

 5:03–6:36

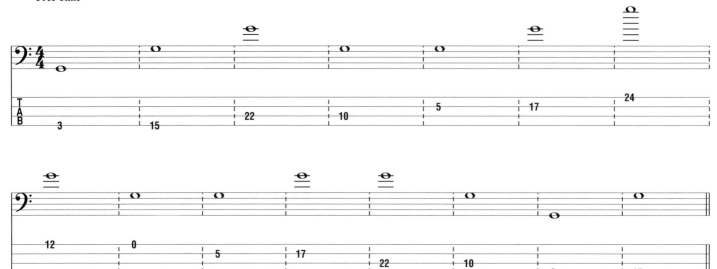

Sliding Exercise for G—Steps #2 and #3:

 6:36–7:16

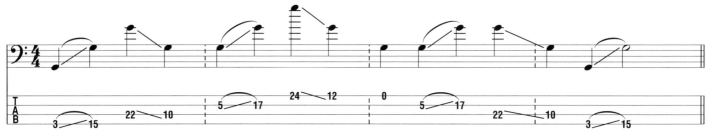

Sliding Exercise for D—Step #1:

▶ 7:16–7:46

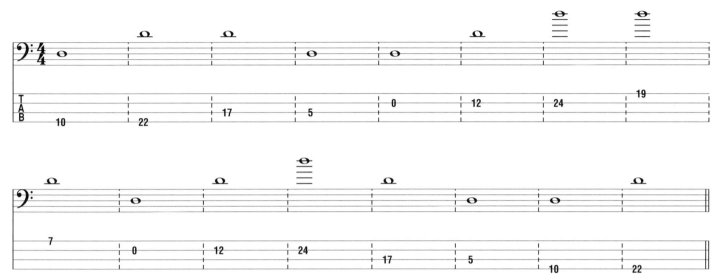

Finish the sliding exercise for the note D (not shown on the video), and then continue on with the remaining notes.

Sliding Exercise for D—Steps #2 and #3:

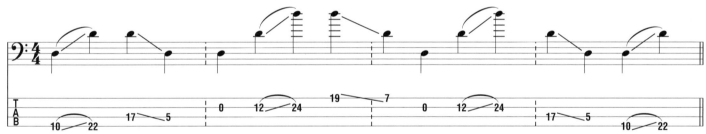

This next exercise will help you to remember the "circle of 5ths" pattern. The order of the notes in the pattern is the same order in which you will practice the notes of the sliding exercise each day (the pattern is also listed over the notes of the exercise).

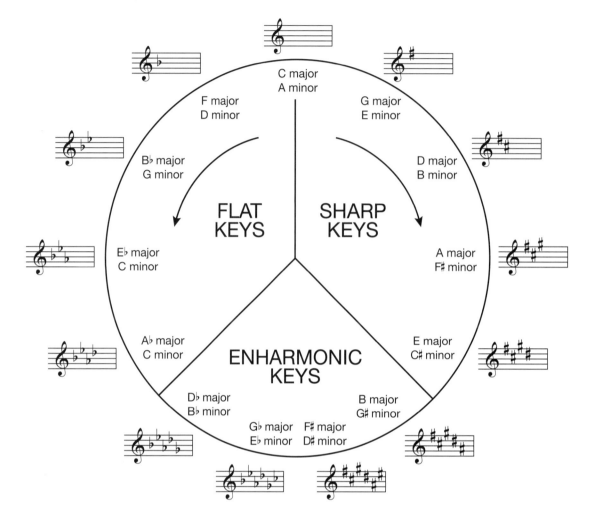

7:46–8:57

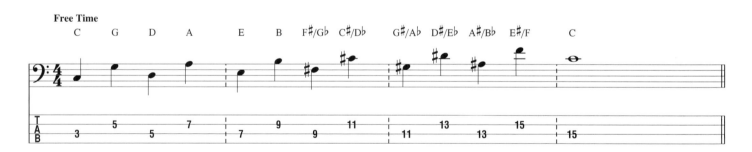

CHAPTER 2

ANALYZING CHORDS

Here is a C major scale pattern in two octaves. The numbers below the tab staff indicate which finger to use for your fretting hand. This will help you to remember the pattern when playing this scale in different areas of the neck.

0:00–1:29

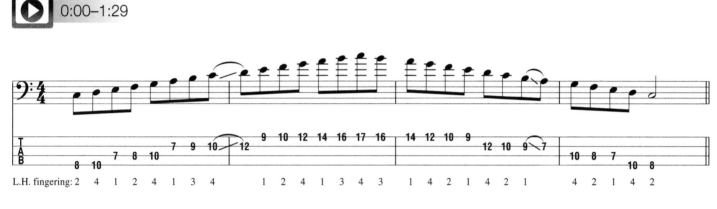

L.H. fingering: 2 4 1 2 4 1 3 4   1 2 4 1 3 4 3   1 4 2 1 4 2 1   4 2 1 4 2

Here is a C minor scale pattern in two octaves:

1:29–1:57

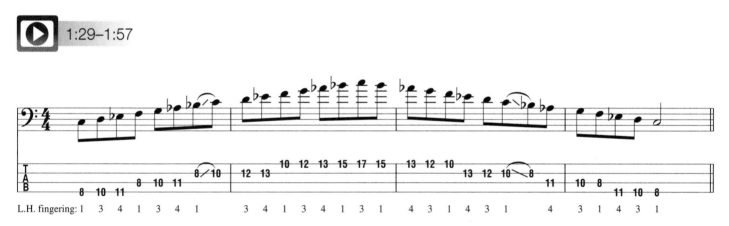

L.H. fingering: 1 3 4 1 3 4 1   3 4 1 3 4 1 3 1   4 3 1 4 3 1   4 3 1 4 3 1

Here is a single-octave interval exercise using the E major scale. As you ascend, memorize the interval shapes and the distance from the root note to each scale degree, all of which are indicated above their respective note.

1:57–3:28

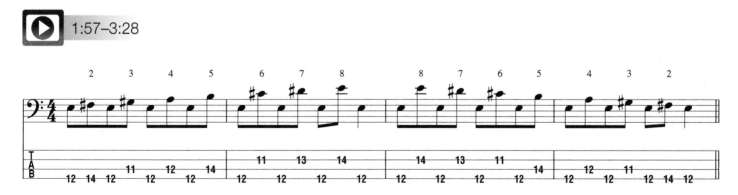

This interval exercise uses the E major scale for the notes in the second octave. Notes that go beyond the first octave of a scale are commonly referred to as "extensions." Once again, each scale degree is indicated over its respective note.

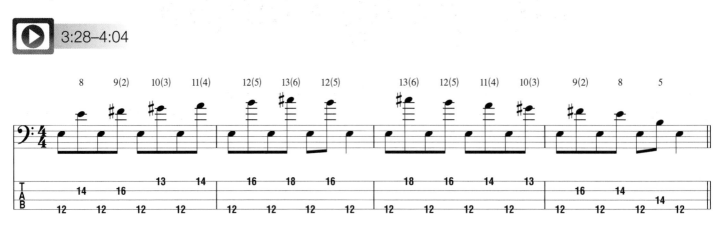

3:28–4:04

CHORD: C

Locate all instances of the C major arpeggio on the fretboard. Each note of the chord is labeled with its correlating scale degree.

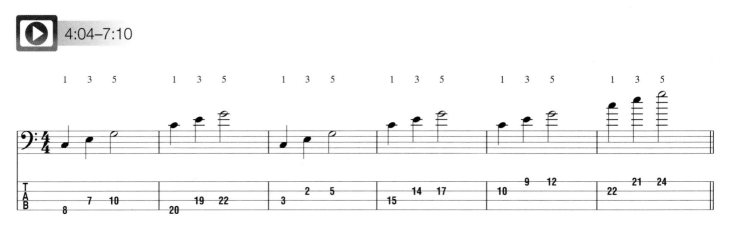

4:04–7:10

CHORD: Cm

Locate all instances of the C minor arpeggio on the fretboard.

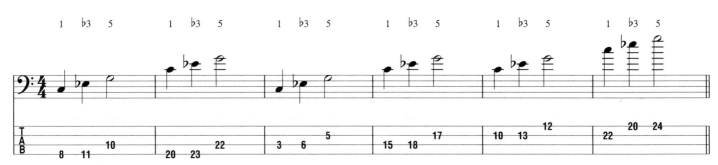

7:10–8:21

CHORD: C7 (also called "C dominant 7")

Locate all instances of the C7 arpeggio on the fretboard.

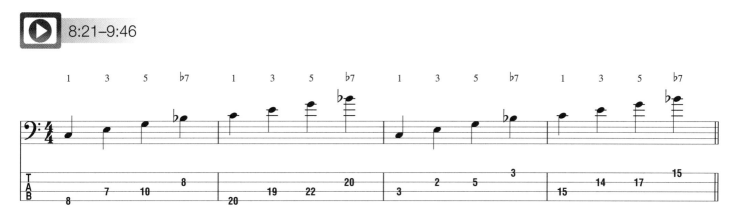

CHORD: Cm♭9

Locate all instances of the Cm♭9 arpeggio on the fretboard. Remember to always convert "extensions" to the first octave by subtracting 7 from the extension's number (9 – 7 = 2). The ♭9th and the ♭2nd are the same note (D♭), just in different octaves. Converting these notes to the first octave allows you to visualize and use the arpeggio shape more effectively. This conversion is also indicated above the notation (along with the other scale degrees).

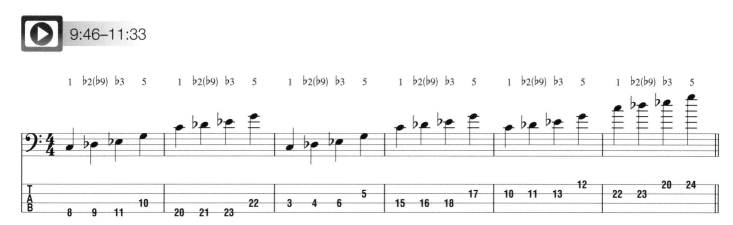

CHORD: Cmaj7♯11

Locate all instances of the Cmaj7♯11 arpeggio on the fretboard.

CHAPTER 3
VOICING CHORDS ON BASS

Practice alternating between these various voicings for the major and minor chord shapes.

 0:00–4:42

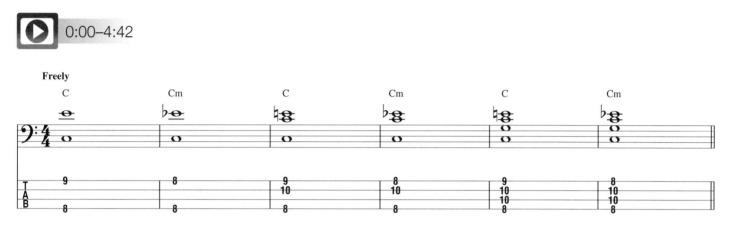

Practice moving the major chord shape around the neck.

 4:42–5:03

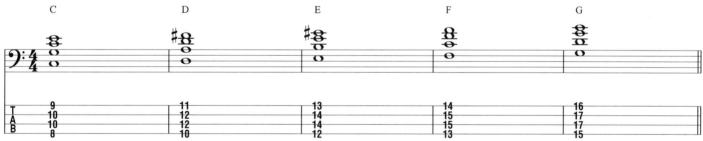

Alternate between the major and minor chord shapes while moving around the neck.

 5:03–5:30

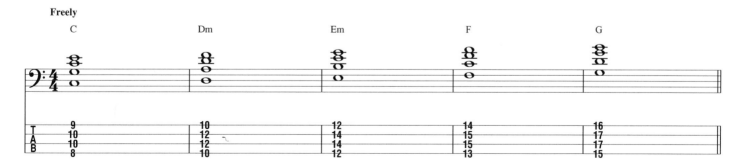

Here are two minor seventh chord voicings:

 5:30–7:09

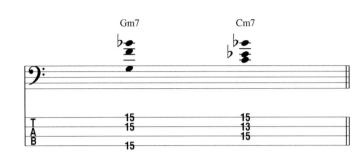

Here are two dominant seventh chord voicings:

 7:09–8:00

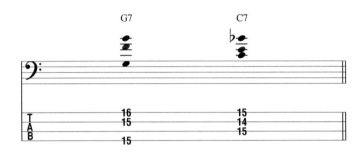

Here are two major seventh chord voicings:

 8:00–8:46

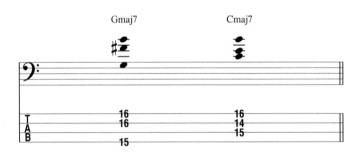

CHAPTER 4
MIXING FRETTED NOTES AND HARMONICS

The following are the most commonly used "harmonic zones" on the bass. Just as you learned the intervals of the scale patterns in Chapter 2, you must learn the harmonics as intervals relative to the note of the open string. This exercise shows each harmonic found on the G string, with the intervallic relationships listed above their respective notes.

 0:00–3:48

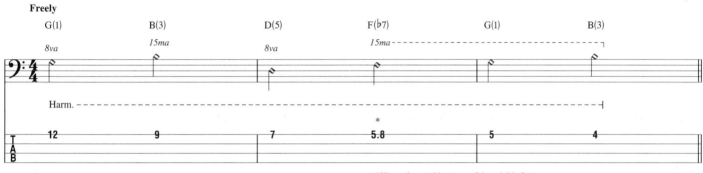

*Harm. located between 5th and 6th frets.

Ten out of the twelve musical notes are available as harmonics on a four-string bass. Play them chromatically to help learn where each note is located, starting with the C harmonic:

 3:48–4:26

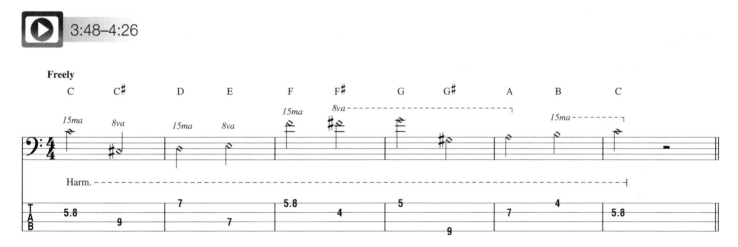

Here are the major and minor 3rd intervals created from each note of the C major scale. The fretted notes serve as the root notes, and the harmonics serve as the major or minor 3rd, depending on the chord quality.

4:26–5:13

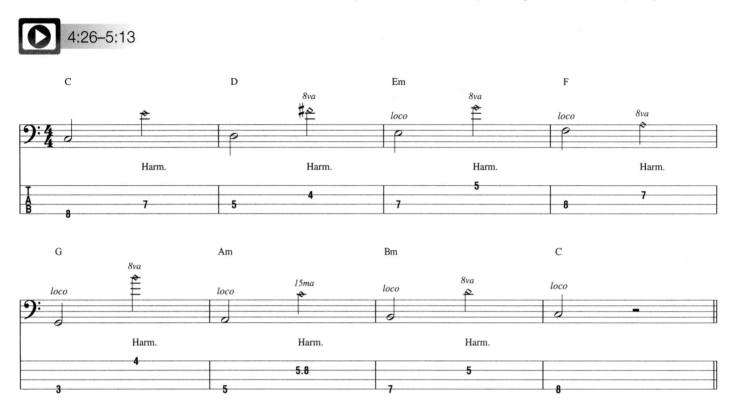

Here are the major and minor triads created from each note of the C major scale. The fretted notes serve as the root notes, and the harmonics serve as the 3rd and 5th of the chord.

5:13–5:48

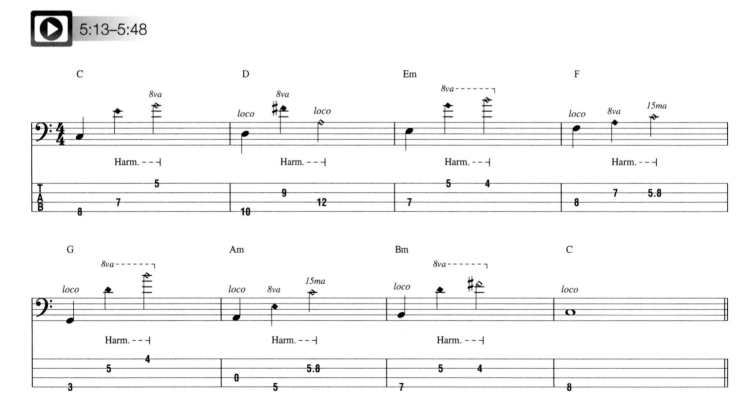

Add harmonics to an existing groove to create a chord. The first line below consists of a basic groove, while the second line adds harmonics over the same groove.

5:48–6:31

Use this groove as the foundation for the next exercise:

6:31–6:55

Now add harmonics to the groove from the previous exercise, utilizing the same chord progression and rhythm. The chords created are listed over each measure.

6:55–7:36

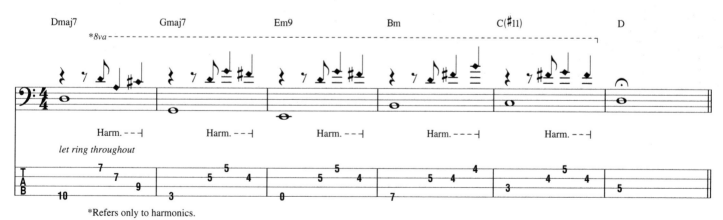

*Refers only to harmonics.

Use this groove as the foundation for the next exercise:

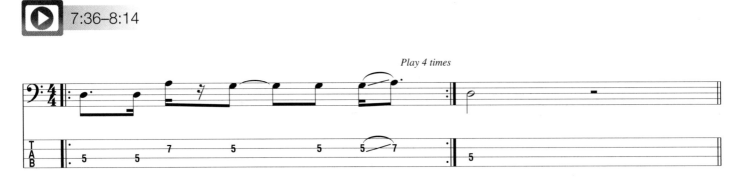

Here, each measure introduces a new harmonic to the groove, starting with the initial groove in measure 1 and ending with the final harmonic-based groove in measure 5.

CHAPTER 5
MIXING CHORDS AND TAPPING

The distance between each note in a major scale is either a whole step (two frets) or a half step (one fret). Once you learn this pattern, you can play the major scale along a single string. In this first example, the distance between each note is listed above the scale.

0:00–2:00

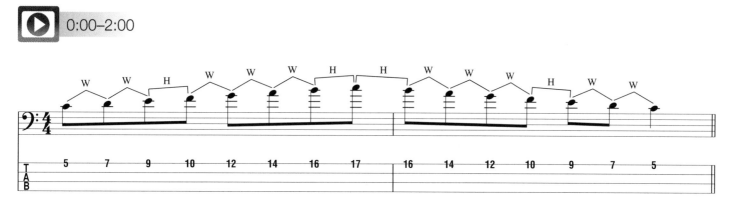

Ascend the C major scale pattern on one string using tapping and pull-offs.

2:00–3:23

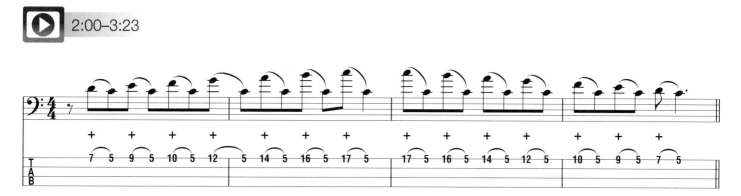

Ascend the C major scale pattern on one string using tapping and pull-offs, starting on A, the sixth degree of the scale.

3:23–4:09

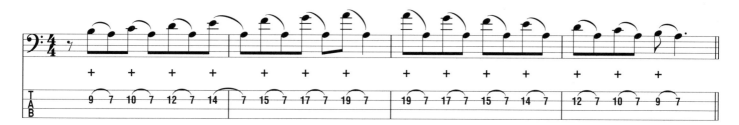

Alternate between each string while ascending the major scale.

▶ 4:09–4:51

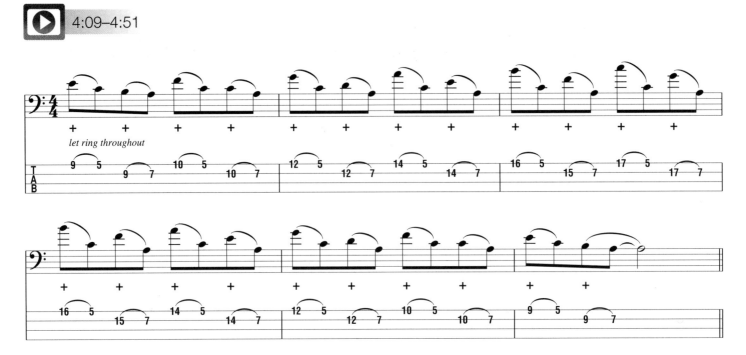

Incorporate a bass fill into the groove using tapping and pull-offs.

▶ 4:51–5:26

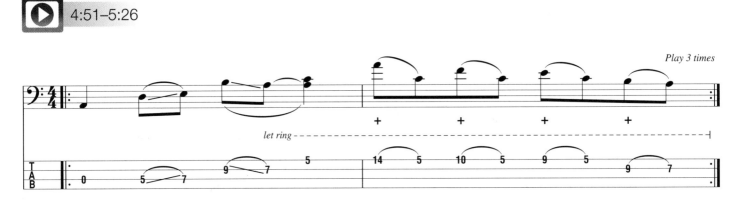

Using the same groove, create a bass fill that utilizes a mixture of tapping, slides, and pull-offs.

▶ 5:26–6:00

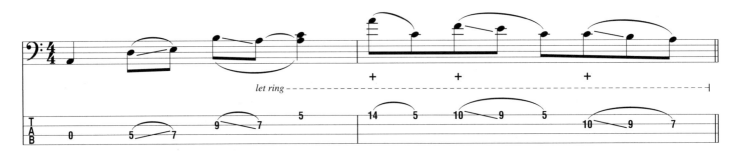

Sustain a C major chord and create a melody using tapping and pull-offs.

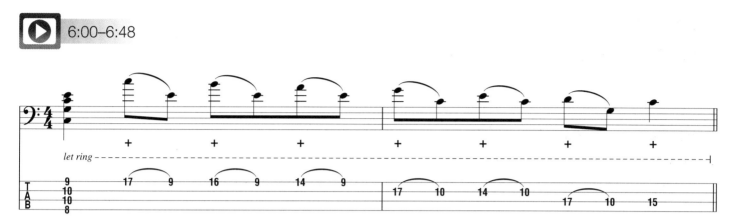

Sustain a C major chord and create a melody using tapping, slides, and pull-offs.

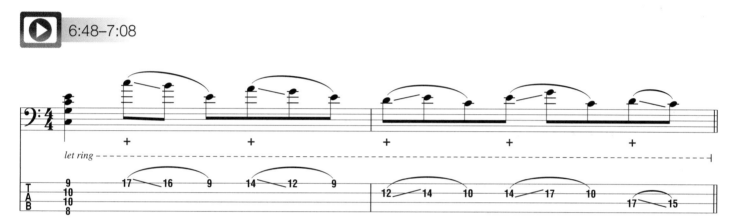

Refer to the accompanying video for this demonstration using tapping, slides, pull-offs, and sustained root notes.

EXPLORING BASS LINE OPTIONS

ABOUT THE BACKING TRACKS

Two versions of each backing track are provided. Use the shorter version to practice the different figures notated in this chapter, and use the extended version to improvise and jam with your own ideas.

BACKING TRACK #1

 0:00–3:30

KEY: E Major
CHORDS: B7add11, A9♯11

NOTE: For this chapter, the chords notated over each bar indicate only the chord progression of the guitar part on the track, not an actual chord being played by the bass. That said, these are the chords from which each bass part is derived. Use the notes contained in each chord to create your own parts when playing along with the downloadable backing tracks included with this book.

3:30–4:24

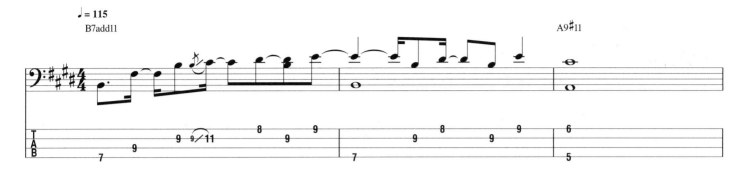

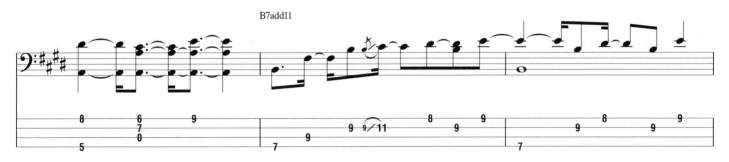

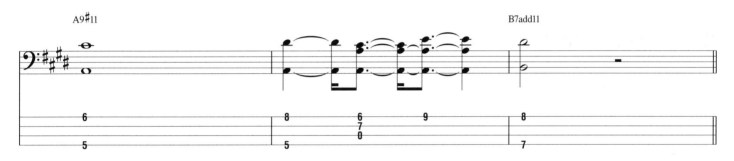

4:24–4:56

*Note is articulated with a legato slide on repeat.

 4:56–5:29

BACKING TRACK #2

 5:30–5:51

KEY: E Minor
CHORDS: Em9, G, D/F♯

TIP: Chords that contain two letters separated by a slash, such as the D/F♯ chord listed above, are "inverted" chords. The first letter in the chord indicates the root of the main chord used (D major), and the second letter is the new bass (lowest) note. Inverted chords are created when the notes of a major triad (D–F♯–A) are arranged in a different order. A first-inversion chord is one in which the 3rd becomes the bass note (F♯–A–D), and a second-inversion chord is one in which the 5th becomes the bass note (A–D–F♯). The chord used in this backing track is a first-inversion D major chord.

 5:51–6:20

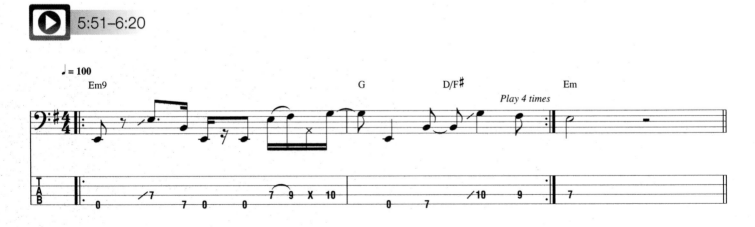

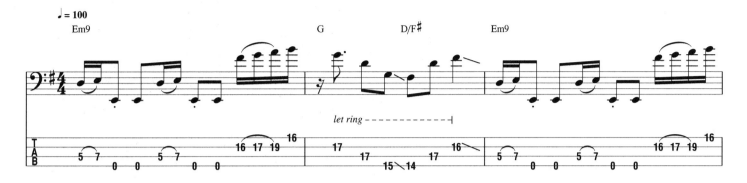

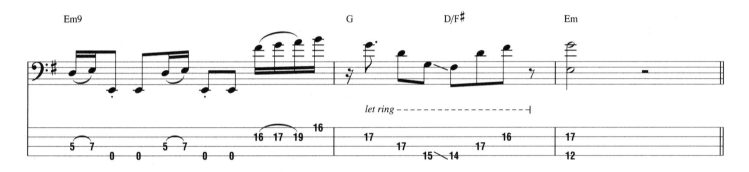

6:52–7:30

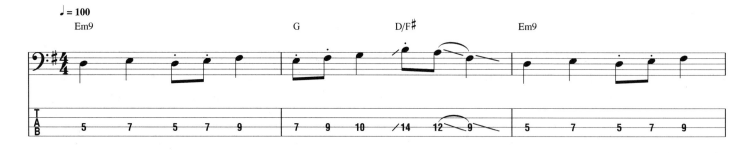

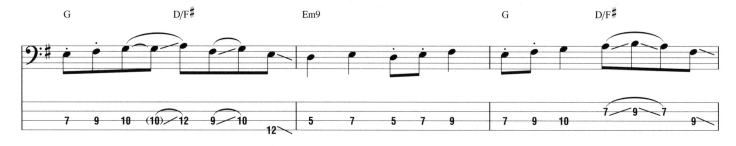

BACKING TRACK #3

 7:30–8:03

KEY: F Major
CHORDS: Gm7, Dm7, C7

 8:03–8:47

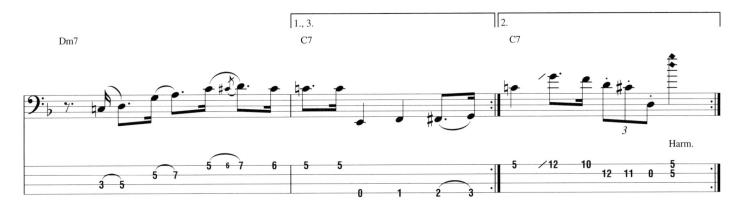

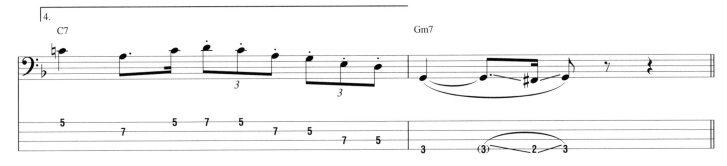

8:47–9:36

9:36–10:25

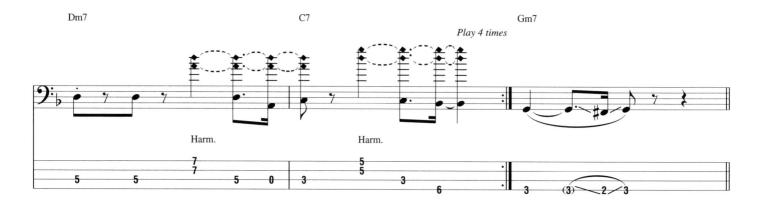

BACKING TRACK #4

 10:25–10:45

KEY: D♭ Major
CHORDS: D♭, B♭m

 10:45–11:17

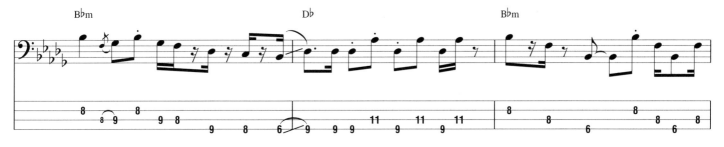

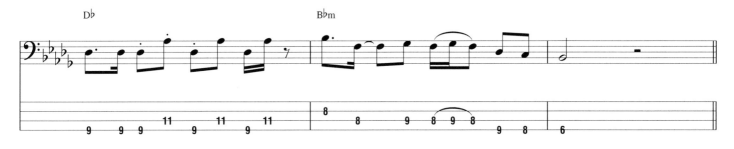

11:17–11:47

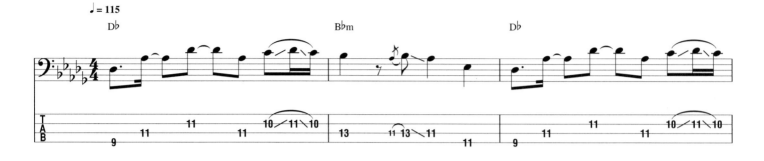

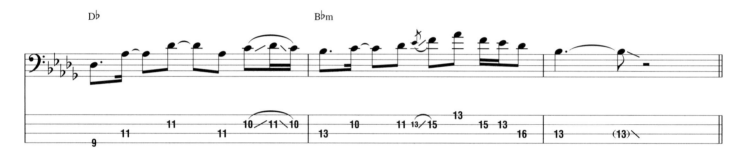

30

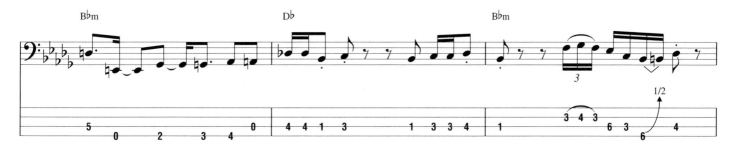

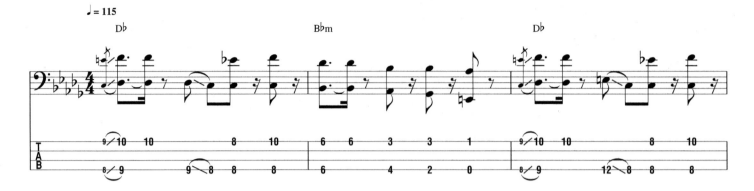

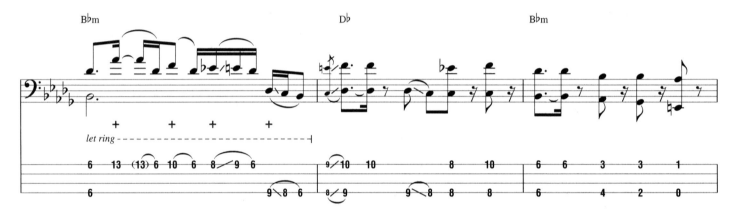

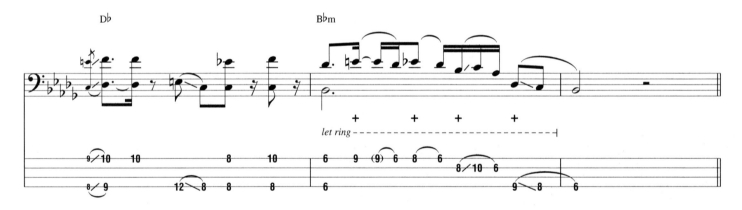

BACKING TRACK #5

 12:56–13:13

KEY: C Major
CHORDS: C11, C9, Am11, Fadd#11, G11

 13:13–13:45

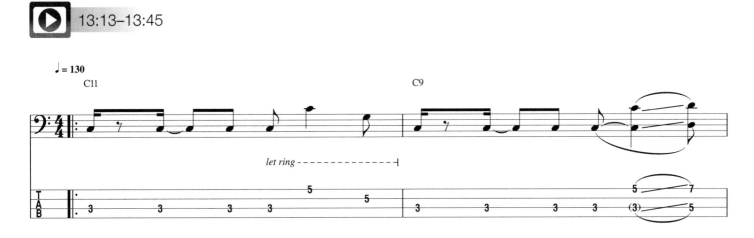

13:45–14:18

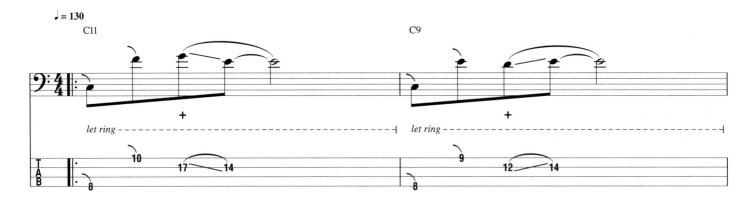

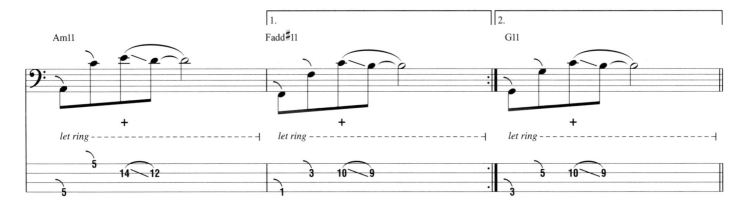

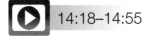

14:18–14:55

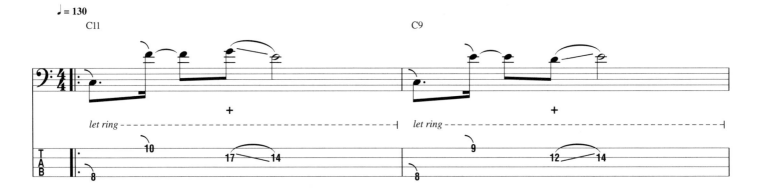

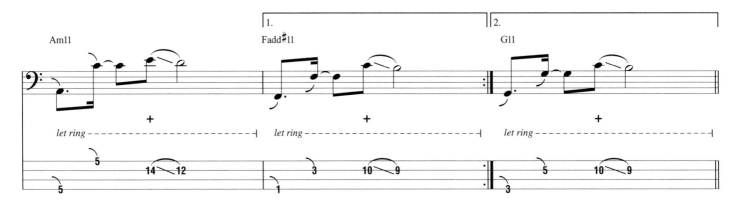

34

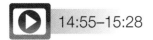

BACKING TRACK #6

 15:28–15:50

KEY: D Major
CHORDS: D, A, Bm, G

 15:50–16:24

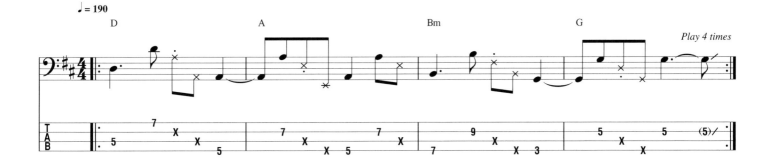

16:24–17:00

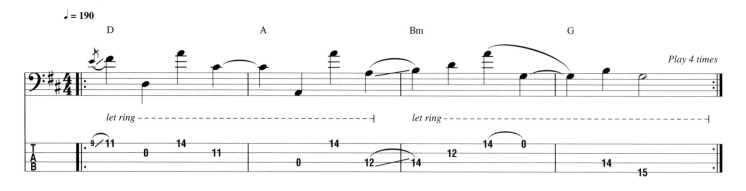

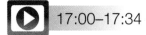17:00–17:34

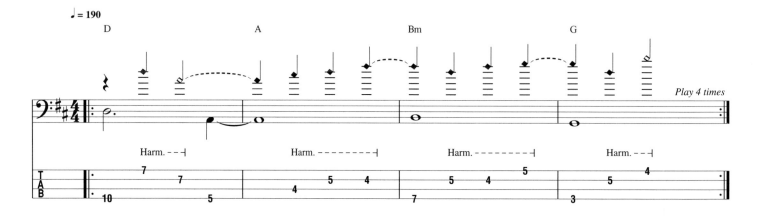

BACKING TRACK #7

 17:34–17:59

KEY: E Minor
CHORDS: Em, F#m(♭5), G, G9, Am11, Bm7, Cmaj7#11

 17:59–18:34

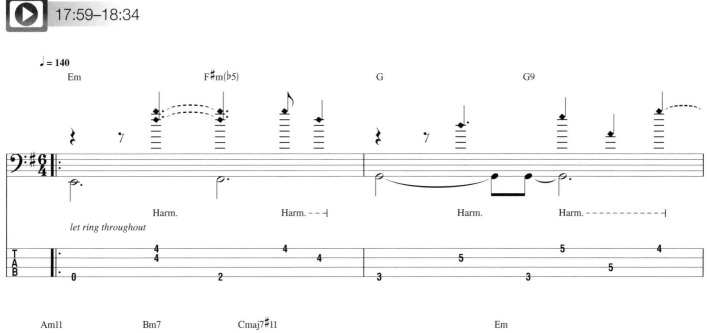

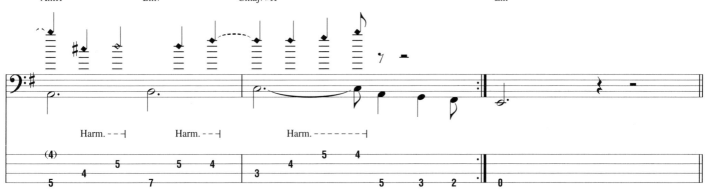

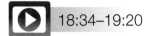 18:34–19:20

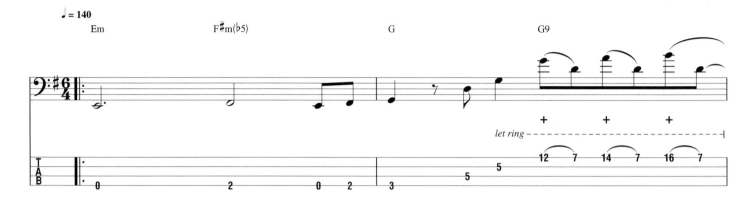

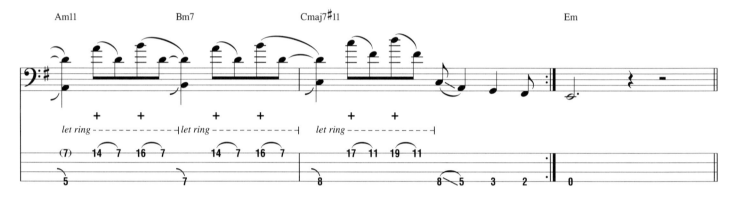

 19:20–19:57

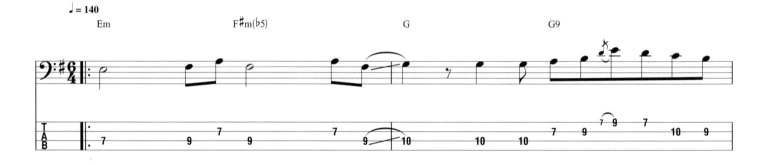

38

BACKING TRACK #8

 19:57–20:19

KEY: F♯ Minor, G Minor
CHORDS: F♯m, Gm

 20:19–20:58

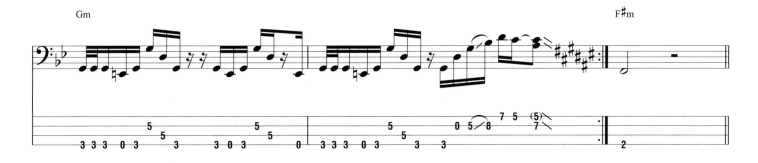

20:58–21:28

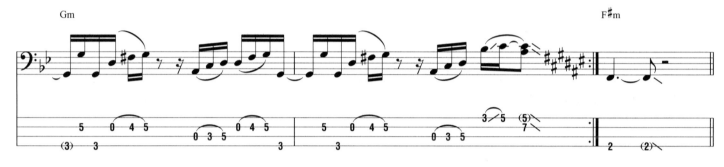

21:28–22:09

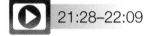

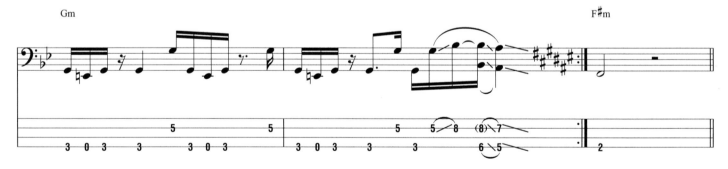

BACKING TRACK #9

KEY: E Minor
CHORDS: Em, G9, Am9

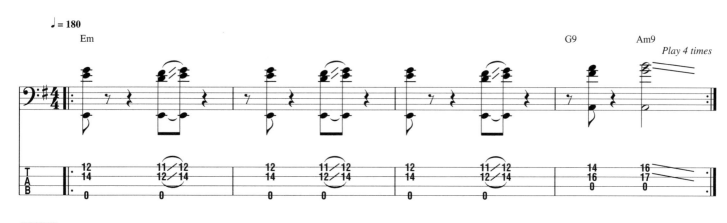

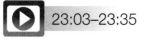

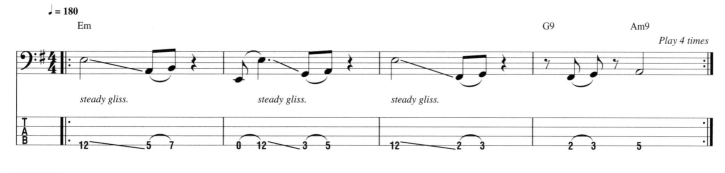

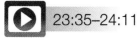

BACKING TRACK #10

 24:11–24:40

KEY: C♯ Minor
CHORDS: C♯m, B, Amaj7, E, F♯m, A9

 24:40–25:19

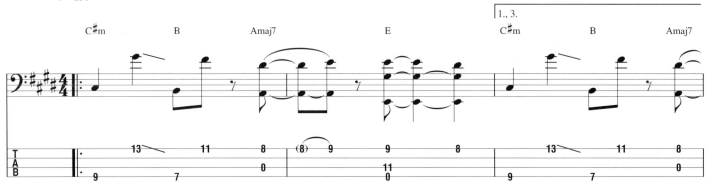

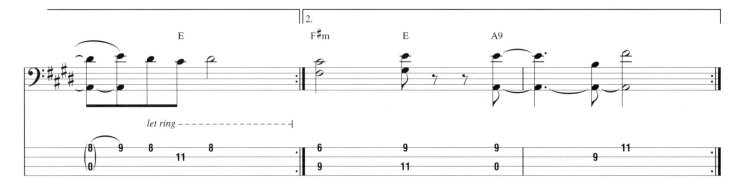

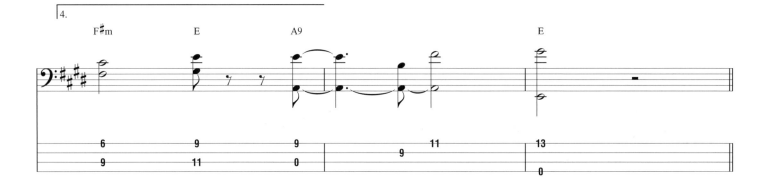

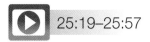

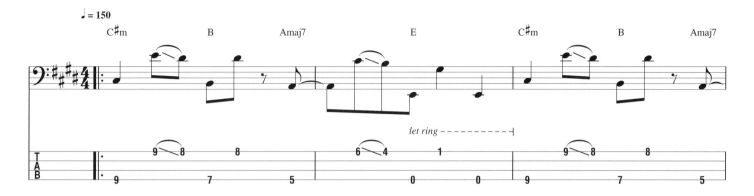

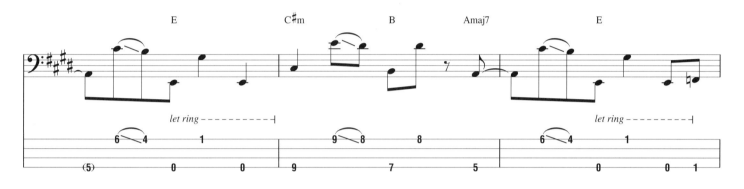

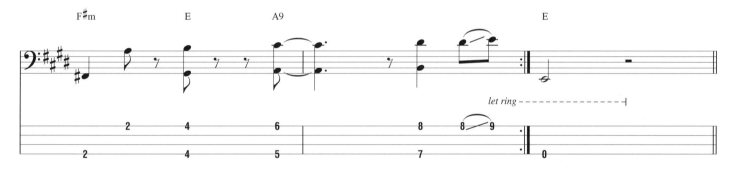

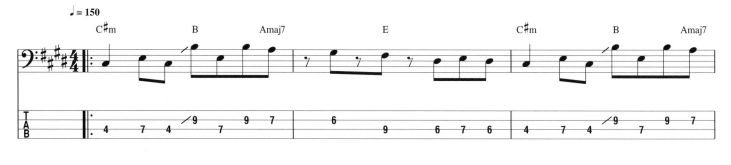

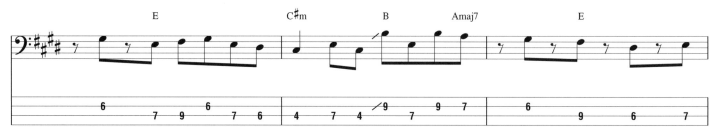

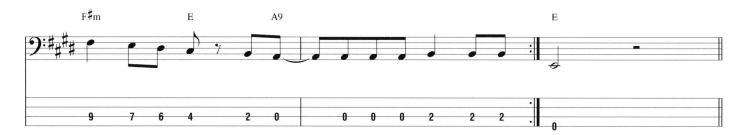

BASS BUILDERS

A series of technique book/CD packages created for the purposeful building and development of your chops. Each volume is written by an expert in that particular technique. And with the inclusion of audio, the added dimension of hearing exactly how to play particular grooves and techniques make these truly like private lessons.

BASS AEROBICS
by Jon Liebman
00696437 Book/Online Audio $19.99

**BASS FITNESS –
AN EXERCISING HANDBOOK**
by Josquin des Prés
00660177.. $10.99

BASS FOR BEGINNERS
by Glenn Letsch
00695099 Book/CD Pack $19.95

BASS GROOVES
by Jon Liebman
00696028 Book/CD Pack $19.99

BASS IMPROVISATION
by Ed Friedland
00695164 Book/CD Pack $17.95

BLUES BASS
by Jon Liebman
00695235 Book/CD Pack $19.95

BUILDING ROCK BASS LINES
by Ed Friedland
00695692 Book/CD Pack $17.95

BUILDING WALKING BASS LINES
by Ed Friedland
00695008 Book/Online Audio $19.99

**RON CARTER –
BUILDING JAZZ BASS LINES**
00841240 Book/CD Pack $19.95

DICTIONARY OF BASS GROOVES
by Sean Malone
00695266 Book/CD Pack $14.95

EXPANDING WALKING BASS LINES
by Ed Friedland
00695026 Book/CD Pack $19.95

**FINGERBOARD HARMONY
FOR BASS**
by Gary Willis
00695043 Book/CD Pack $17.95

FUNK BASS
by Jon Liebman
00699348 Book/CD Pack $19.99

FUNK/FUSION BASS
by Jon Liebman
00696553 Book/CD Pack $19.95

HIP-HOP BASS
by Josquin des Prés
00695589 Book/CD Pack................................... $14.95

JAZZ BASS
by Ed Friedland
00695084 Book/Online Audio $17.99

**JERRY JEMMOTT –
BLUES AND RHYTHM &
BLUES BASS TECHNIQUE**
00695176 Book/CD Pack................................... $17.95

JUMP 'N' BLUES BASS
by Keith Rosier
00695292 Book/CD Pack................................... $16.95

**THE LOST ART OF
COUNTRY BASS**
by Keith Rosier
00695107 Book/CD Pack................................... $19.95

**PENTATONIC SCALES
FOR BASS**
by Ed Friedland
00696224 Book/CD Pack................................... $19.99

REGGAE BASS
by Ed Friedland
00695163 Book/CD Pack................................... $16.95

'70S FUNK & DISCO BASS
by Josquin des Prés
00695614 Book/CD Pack................................... $15.99

**SIMPLIFIED SIGHT-READING
FOR BASS**
by Josquin des Prés
00695085 Book/CD Pack................................... $17.95

6-STRING BASSICS
by David Gross
00695221 Book/CD Pack................................... $12.95

**WORLD BEAT GROOVES
FOR BASS**
by Tony Cimorosi
00695335 Book/CD Pack................................... $14.95

**HAL•LEONARD®
CORPORATION**
7777 W. BLUEMOUND RD. P.O. BOX 13819 MILWAUKEE, WI 53213

Visit Hal Leonard Online at **www.halleonard.com**

Prices, contents and availability subject to change without notice; All prices are listed in U.S. funds

0915

HAL•LEONARD BASS PLAY-ALONG

The Bass Play-Along™ Series will help you play your favorite songs quickly and easily! Just follow the tab, listen to the CD or online audio to hear how the bass should sound, and then play along using the separate backing tracks. The melody and lyrics are also included in the book in case you want to sing, or to simply help you follow along. The audio files are enhanced so you can adjust the recording to any tempo without changing pitch!

1. Rock
00699674 Book/CD Pack..............................$12.95

2. R&B
00699675 Book/CD Pack..............................$14.99

3. Pop/Rock
00699677 Book/CD Pack..............................$12.95

4. '90s Rock
00699679 Book/CD Pack..............................$12.95

5. Funk
00699680 Book/CD Pack..............................$12.95

6. Classic Rock
00699678 Book/CD Pack..............................$12.95

7. Hard Rock
00699676 Book/CD Pack..............................$14.95

9. Blues
00699817 Book/CD Pack..............................$14.99

10. Jimi Hendrix Smash Hits
00699815 Book/CD Pack..............................$17.99

11. Country
00699818 Book/CD Pack..............................$12.95

12. Punk Classics
00699814 Book/CD Pack..............................$12.99

13. Lennon & McCartney
00699816 Book/CD Pack..............................$14.99

14. Modern Rock
00699821 Book/CD Pack..............................$14.99

15. Mainstream Rock
00699822 Book/CD Pack..............................$14.99

16. '80s Metal
00699825 Book/CD Pack..............................$16.99

17. Pop Metal
00699826 Book/CD Pack..............................$14.99

18. Blues Rock
00699828 Book/CD Pack..............................$14.99

19. Steely Dan
00700203 Book/CD Pack..............................$16.99

20. The Police
00700270 Book/CD Pack..............................$14.99

21. Rock Band – Modern Rock
00700705 Book/CD Pack..............................$14.95

22. Rock Band – Classic Rock
00700706 Book/CD Pack..............................$14.95

23. Pink Floyd – Dark Side of The Moon
00700847 Book/CD Pack..............................$14.99

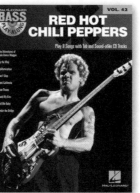

24. Weezer
00700960 Book/CD Pack..............................$14.99

25. Nirvana
00701047 Book/CD Pack..............................$14.99

26. Black Sabbath
00701180 Book/CD Pack..............................$16.99

27. Kiss
00701181 Book/CD Pack..............................$14.99

28. The Who
00701182 Book/CD Pack..............................$14.99

29. Eric Clapton
00701183 Book/CD Pack..............................$14.99

30. Early Rock
00701184 Book/CD Pack..............................$15.99

31. The 1970s
00701185 Book/CD Pack..............................$14.99

33. Christmas Hits
00701197 Book/CD Pack..............................$12.99

34. Easy Songs
00701480 Book/CD Pack..............................$12.99

35. Bob Marley
00701702 Book/CD Pack..............................$14.99

36. Aerosmith
00701886 Book/CD Pack..............................$14.99

37. Modern Worship
00701920 Book/CD Pack..............................$12.99

38. Avenged Sevenfold
00702386 Book/CD Pack..............................$16.99

40. AC/DC
14041594 Book/CD Pack..............................$16.99

41. U2
00702582 Book/CD Pack..............................$16.99

42. Red Hot Chili Peppers
00702991 Book/CD Pack..............................$19.99

43. Paul McCartney
00703079 Book/CD Pack..............................$17.99

44. Megadeth
00703080 Book/CD Pack..............................$16.99

45. Slipknot
00703201 Book/CD Pack..............................$16.99

46. Best Bass Lines Ever
00103359 Book/Online Audio..........................$17.99

48. James Brown
00117421 Book/CD Pack..............................$16.99

49. Eagles
00119936 Book/CD Pack..............................$17.99

51. Stevie Ray Vaughan
00146154 Book/Online Audio..........................$16.99

FOR MORE INFORMATION, SEE YOUR LOCAL MUSIC DEALER, OR WRITE TO:

HAL•LEONARD® CORPORATION
7777 W. BLUEMOUND RD. P.O. BOX 13819 MILWAUKEE, WI 53213

Prices, contents, and availability subject to change without notice.

Visit Hal Leonard Online at **www.halleonard.com**

0515

BASS RECORDED VERSIONS

Bass Recorded Versions
feature authentic transcriptions
written in standard notation
and tablature for bass guitar.
This series features complete
bass lines from the classics
to contemporary superstars.

**25 All-Time
Rock Bass Classics**
00690445 / $14.95

**25 Essential
Rock Bass Classics**
00690210 / $15.95

**Avenged Sevenfold –
Nightmare**
00691054 / $19.99

Bass Tab 1990-1999
00690400 / $16.95

Bass Tab 1999-2000
00690404 / $14.95

Bass Tab 2013
00121899 / $19.99

Bass Tab White Pages
00690508 / $29.99

The Beatles – Abbey Road
00128336 / $22.99

The Beatles Bass Lines
00690170 / $14.95

The Beatles 1962-1966
00690556 / $18.99

The Beatles 1967-1970
00690557 / $19.99

The Best of Blink 182
00690549 / $18.95

Best of Bass Tab
00141806 / $14.99

Blues Bass Classics
00690291 / $14.95

Boston Bass Collection
00690935 / $19.95

The Best of Eric Clapton
00660187 / $19.95

Stanley Clarke Collection
00672307 / $19.95

**Dream Theater
Bass Anthology**
00119345 / $24.99

Funk Bass Bible
00690744 / $19.95

Hard Rock Bass Bible
00690746 / $17.95

**Jimi Hendrix –
Are You Experienced?**
00690371 / $17.95

Incubus – Morning View
00690639 / $17.95

**Iron Maiden Bass
Anthology**
00690867 / $22.99

Jazz Bass Classics
00102070 / $17.99

Best of Kiss for Bass
00690080 / $19.95

**Lynyrd Skynyrd –
All-Time Greatest Hits**
00690956 / $19.99

Bob Marley Bass Collection
00690568 / $19.95

Mastodon – Crack the Skye
00691007 / $19.99

Megadeth Bass Anthology
00691191 / $19.99

Metal Bass Tabs
00103358 / $19.99

Best of Marcus Miller
00690811 / $24.99

Motown Bass Classics
00690253 / $14.95

Muse Bass Tab Collection
00123275 / $19.99

Nirvana Bass Collection
00690066 / $19.95

No Doubt – Tragic Kingdom
00120112 / $22.95

**The Offspring –
Greatest Hits**
00690809 / $17.95

**Jaco Pastorius –
Greatest Jazz Fusion
Bass Player**
00690421 / $19.99

The Essential Jaco Pastorius
00690420 / $19.99

Pearl Jam – Ten
00694882 / $16.99

**Pink Floyd –
Dark Side of the Moon**
00660172 / $14.95

The Best of Police
00660207 / $14.95

Pop/Rock Bass Bible
00690747 / $17.95

Queen – The Bass Collection
00690065 / $19.99

R&B Bass Bible
00690745 / $17.95

Rage Against the Machine
00690248 / $17.99

**The Best of
Red Hot Chili Peppers**
00695285 / $24.95

**Red Hot Chili Peppers –
Blood Sugar Sex Magik**
00690064 / $19.95

**Red Hot Chili Peppers –
By the Way**
00690585 / $19.95

**Red Hot Chili Peppers –
Californication**
00690390 / $19.95

**Red Hot Chili Peppers –
Greatest Hits**
00690675 / $18.95

**Red Hot Chili Peppers –
I'm with You**
00691167 / $22.99

**Red Hot Chili Peppers –
One Hot Minute**
00690091 / $18.95

**Red Hot Chili Peppers –
Stadium Arcadium**
00690853 / $24.95

**Red Hot Chili Peppers –
Stadium Arcadium:
Deluxe Edition**
Book/2-CD Pack
00690863 / $39.95

Rock Bass Bible
00690446 / $19.95

Rolling Stones
00690256 / $16.95

**Sly & The Family Stone
for Bass**
00109733 / $19.99

**Stevie Ray Vaughan –
Lightnin' Blues 1983-1987**
00694778 / $19.95

Best of Yes
00103044 / $19.99

Best of ZZ Top for Bass
00691069 / $22.99

HAL•LEONARD®
CORPORATION

7777 W. BLUEMOUND RD. P.O. BOX 13819 MILWAUKEE, WI 53213

Visit Hal Leonard Online at
www.halleonard.com

Prices, contents & availability subject to change without notice.
Some products may not be available outside the U.S.A.

1015